Riffs & Improvisations

Riffs & Improvisations

Poems by

Gregory Luce

Cover design by Shay Culligan

ISBN: 978-1-63980-015-5

Kelsay Books
502 South 1040 East, A-119
American Fork, Utah 84003
Kelsaybooks.com

for Naomi, Alex, Theo, and the ancestors

Acknowledgments

"Music to It" first appeared in *Wordgathering*

"An air that kills" first appeared in *Mad Rush*

"Satie in the Dark" first appeared in *Mile Nine*

"Improvisation: 'Better git it in your soul'" first appeared in
  Logical Reader 1997

"Sphere" first appeared in *Shades of Gray*

"Improvisation: Sunk"first appeared in *Nebo*

"And She Moves" first appeared in *Broadkill Review*

"Lush Life" first appeared in *Maryland Literary Review*

"Aspirins and Coffee" first appeared in *Little Patuxent Review*

"Music to It" first appeared in *Wordgathering*

"Tranesque" first appeared in *Juke Jar;* reprinted 2019 in
  Derelict Lit

"Satie in the Dark" first appeared in *Nine Mile*

"Return to a Love Supreme" first appeared in *Gargoyle*

"Dark Was the Night" first appeared in *The Dead Mule School of
  Southern Literature*

Contents

Music is feeling, then, not sound;
And thus it is that what I feel,
Here in this room, desiring you...
Is music.
—Wallace Stevens

Music to It

If I could just put music to it
this feeling that drives me
through the Metro station
wanting to dance and glide
like a disembodied spirit
seen and not seen
between all these other bodies.
Or this other feeling of enclosure
in a transparent cocoon,
coiled tight, my camera eye grasping
and drawing in every image. Every
song that jumps through my earphones
from Counting Crows to Sparklehorse
to Badly Drawn Boy perfectly frames
its moment but then dissolves into the next,
and I can't sit still, fingers and toes
tapping, shoulders swaying, I feel
my body hurtling through space
at the speed of the train, until
it shudders to a stop. I take
a deep breath as I exit the car,
walk quivering toward the exit,
one last song pulsing against
the inside of my head.

"An air that kills"

Music drifts into the night air
and catches my ear and I pause
as the melody takes shape
and brings a thought
just deep enough for tears.
We danced to this tune
once—and that one time enough—
so long ago and long forgotten
until now and your eyes
shine again and I hear
you whisper underneath
the song, a memory
that pricks without
the power to console.

(The title is taken from a poem by A.E. Housman.)

Perhaps a dance…

a simple two-step
with just our fingertips
touching and my hand
very light on your
back and if you
gently placed your
hand on my shoulder
we could sweep each
other along in lazy
circles around the
floor and if just
by chance you pressed
your cheek to mine
and rested your head
against my neck and
I caught the scent
of your hair
and pulled your body
a little more tightly
against me and I
couldn't for a moment
tell your breathing from
mine or precisely where
my leg ended and yours
began and you whispered
something into my ear
and everything but the
music and our dancing
and our breathing
stopped….

And She Moves

(After Nick Cave / for Naomi)

And she moves among small birds
and seed falls from her hand
like droplets from the fingers
of Aphrodite in a fountain
And she moves like a shadow
and light trickles from her fingertips
like grains of wheat scattering in the wind
And something inside me sinks deep and rises
and birds skitter from the shadows
sprinkling dust and sunlight
and I am stilled, trembling.

Improvisation: Sunk

(Inspired by Andrew Bird's "Lusitania")

We didn't really meet,
we collided, but somehow
the parts fused into a ship
that sailed erratically,
never arriving at port,
taking on water,
always listing dangerously.
Our affair was the *Lusitania:*
That torpedo had our names
on it from the start.

Piano

Somewhere a piano
is playing muffled
a breath suspended
in the air
between us so cold
I can only touch
you with gloved
fingers.

Now smoke rises from
my mouth and the pipe
burns my fingers.

Somewhere down the hall
a phone rings in
an empty apartment.

Satie in the Dark

Gymnopédie No. 1 emanates
from the speakers, oscillates
through the room and into
my ears. I turned out
the light so I wouldn't
feel alone and though
I know what's coming
so I can see better.
The faces crowd
out of the dark, one
by one they array
themselves before me:
old lovers, my dead—
my father and mother
and the others—oh
how they crowd around—
my own face aging
year by year. And then
the recent places:
the hospitals, waiting
rooms, doctors' offices—
all in a three-and-a-half minute
silent movie. I shiver
and blink, and rub my eyes
and the phantoms vanish
as the next tune starts to play.

Richard Strauss in Purgatory

...we are both at rest from our wanderings / now above the quiet land.
   —Joseph von Eichendorff, Im Abendrot, text for the fourth of the
     Letzte Lieder

It's colder here than I'd imagined.
I seem to be in the waiting room—
Perhaps I can still plead my case,
if not for Heaven at least for the First Circle.
I was a sort of pagan after all. I think
Herr Hitler intuited that from my *Zarathustra,*
and though of course he did grotesquely
misconstrue it as he did Nietzsche's,
he at least knew the value of my work.
I was not unvirtuous. Though the bureaucracy here
is no doubt even worse than the Nazis'.
How I despised their Jew-baiting, Jew-hating,
scapegoating of those vastly more cultured
than they could ever hope to be.

Yet how could I refuse to take the *Reichsmusikkammer?*
It was only to preserve the work of Mahler,
Debussy, Mendelssohn, and then there was
my beloved Zweig whose friendship I kept
and treasured even after my letter to him cost me
my position, thanks to the machinations
of that malignant dwarf Goebbels,
even after those degenerates drove him
to Brazil and suicide. How else but by
cooperating could I have saved my dearest
daughter-in-law Alice twice and my son with her?
By God, didn't I drive to the very gates
of Theresienstadt and plead for the release

of Alice's grandmother Frau Neumann?
Did I not risk my own skin with the SS
in trying to rescue her siblings?
Of course I kept composing—What else
could I do? And yes, naturally, I let
them have my *Olympische Hymne.*
The world would be there after all,
and better they hear my work, expressive
of *der echter Deutscher Geist,* than some
kitsch from one of Goebbels' approved
mediocrities.

Should I perhaps have fled
to California like Mann and sat in the sun
flinging criticism from that safe distance?
Who was he to judge after his flirtation
with Communism? Yes, I did sign that manifesto
denouncing him, but what choice did I have
if I wanted to go on living and composing
and protecting what family members I could?
It isn't as if that piece of paper did him
any harm.

I withdrew to the mountains
as soon as I decently could. Thank God
the first American soldiers to arrive
were serious musicians, and they knew my work.
I hardly expected Americans to be so cultured.
It was simple courtesy—*nein*—gratitude that prompted
me to write my Oboe Concerto for them. Anything
to accommodate the new masters of the world,
nicht wahr?

I wrote my *Vier Letzte Lieder*
as a kind of expiation, an attempt to give
the world unrequested beauty that demands
nothing in return but open ears.
Have I failed even at that? May I not
finally have rest from my wanderings?

Improvisation: "Better git it in your soul"

(for Jim)

Better embrace it like Mingus'
bass, stroke it, caress it, pull it in,
draw it like smoke, drink it
like old bourbon burning
all the way down.
Then give it back.

Double Bass

(for H.S.)

The plucked notes of the bass
mimic my heartbeats and then
the bow draws out a long
low moan the way your hand did
drawn across my back.

Dark Was the Night

Haints are afoot
as Blind Willie Johnson
sidles out of Waco
without eyes he sees
shadows black as the night sky,
haints sliding along
the cold graveyard ground
like a penknife down the neck
of a battered guitar.

Mystère

The ghost of Erik Satie
hovers over the keyboard
where Monk's huge hands
reach for the infinite,
grasping at chords that seem
humanly impossible. A breeze
from Paris 1920 wafts
over the piano. Monk mops
his forehead. Somewhere
Satie is smiling.

Sphere

(for Reuben Jackson)

Misterioso? Yes,
like a gray cat
at night jumping
into and out of
a sliver of light
on the sidewalk.
Misterioso, yes, the way
big raindrops hit
a metal roof, pool
and slide down
in spatters and
rivulets.
The way hot oil
jumps and pops
its rhythms
in the skillet.
Yes, misterioso
like a walk in the night
through New York,
New Orleans,
Paris, or your city or
mine when the sounds
and smells and flavors
flow and dance around
you and the feeling is, yes,
misterioso.

Bill Evans Suite

1. *Waltz for Debby*
2. *B Minor Waltz (for Ellaine)*
3. *The Two Lonely People*
4. *Like Someone in Love*
5. *You Must Believe in Spring*

1. The fingers move lightly
across the keys, light-footed
notes three-stepping up
and sideways like a heart
with an extra beat, inside
my chest another waltz.

2. Another waltz for someone
lost, a heart stopped under
the wheels that moved horribly
unlike fingers rolling gently
along the keyboard, two hands
finding and not finding each other.

3. Finding and not finding
each other, drinking together
from the same lonely spring,
slaking the same thirst that
one drop from the tip of your
tongue could slake.

4. Your tongue slakes
my thirst drop by drop
until the spring runs dry
in summer's heat.

5. Even in summer's heat
spring lingers. We seek
refreshment from those sources
we can find, even in summer's
heat believing in spring.

Lush Life

It has to be Johnny Hartman
with Trane framing that
voice that flows smooth
and rich like a river
of barrel proof bourbon
rippling with McCoy's chords,
Jimmy and Elvin's beats
popping like ice in a glass,
and the wheel of life starts
rolling you back through
the gay places, the low
dives, finally the side porch,
sitting alone late at night,
that pint bottle at your feet
almost exhaling whiskey breath,
you running your finger
around the rim of the glass,
tracing each bead of sweat
sliding down the sides,
pressing it to your forehead
to cool the sudden flush
that starts just at the hairline,
hands trembling a little now,
so another small splash into
the glass, slivers of ice tinkling
as your hand shakes,
the lush life in this small
circle of light.

Aspirins and Coffee

and Coltrane on the stereo
a glass of water sweats beads in the dead center of the
        kitchen table
dust motes dazzle in a single bar of morning sunlight
"a Love Supreme a Love Supreme"
fingers drum on the edge of the table and push the pills
        from side to side
my heart pulses ragged against the inside of my chest
my breath comes sharp and jagged
"a Love Supreme a Love Supreme"
Jimmy's bass notes step up my spine and thump
        the base of my skull
Elvin's sticks tattoo the back of my head from the inside
McCoy's chords shatter like fine crystal behind my eyes
"a Love Supreme a Love Supreme"
and then Trane's lines burn up from my gut like raw liquid sugar
        like hot syrup like pure honey
"a Love Supreme a Love Supreme"
and I am quivering now my head throbs and pulses and
        my stomach clenches
                "a Love Supreme a Love Supreme"
sunlight washes over the table and I am grasping at the edge
slowly I loosen my grip and lay my head down sideways, close
        my eyes in the light of a love supreme.

Tranesque

(for Moira)

The very thought of you
after one long evening
of talk cascades
through my mind
like music, like
your hair over
your shoulders
in the flickering
candlelight as the breeze
grew chill and your voice
came warm across
the small space between
us, your words,
too, cascading like
notes, like Trane
soloing filigrees.

Return to A Love Supreme

(after Chasing Trane)

The stairs to heaven
are uneven some broken
you go sideways sometimes
take a step down for
every two up but you climb
and stumble always
grasping the pure beam
of light that he sends back
from somewhere he is
always up ahead.
I try to work my pen
for Trane the way
he played his sax
for God.

About the Author

Gregory Luce is the author of the chapbooks *Signs of Small Grace* (Pudding House Publications) and *Drinking Weather* (Finishing Line Press), the collection *Memory and Desire* (Sweatshoppe Publications), and the chapbook *Tile,* (Finishing Line). His poems have appeared in numerous print and online journals, including *Kansas Quarterly, Cimarron Review, Innisfree Poetry Review, Northern Virginia Review, Foundling Review, MiPOesias, Little Patuxent Review, Words Dance, Rising Tide Review, Wordgathering, Faircloth Review, Broadkill Review, Bourgeon, Deaf Poets Society, Maryland Poetry Review, Mile Nine,* and in the anthologies *Living in Storms* (Eastern Washington University Press), *Bigger Than They Appear* (Accents Publishing), and *Unrequited: An Anthology of Love Poems about Inanimate Objects.* In 2014, he was awarded the Larry Neal Award for adult poetry by the D.C. Commission on the Arts and Humanities. He is retired from the National Geographic Society, volunteers as a writing tutor/mentor for 826DC, and lives in Arlington, VA.